Violin for Kids

How to Play, Master the Basics and Create Beautiful Melodies

© **Copyright 2024 - All rights reserved.**

The content contained within this book may not be reproduced, duplicated, or transmitted without direct written permission from the author or the publisher.

Under no circumstances will any blame or legal responsibility be held against the publisher or author for any damages, reparation, or monetary loss due to the information contained within this book, either directly or indirectly.

Legal Notice:

This book is copyright-protected. It is only for personal use. You cannot amend, distribute, sell, use, quote, or paraphrase any part of the content within this book without the consent of the author or publisher.

Disclaimer Notice:

Please note the information contained within this document is for educational and entertainment purposes only. All effort has been executed to present accurate, up-to-date, reliable, and complete information. No warranties of any kind are declared or implied. Readers acknowledge that the author is not engaging in the rendering of legal, financial, medical, or professional advice. The content within this book has been derived from various sources. Please consult a licensed professional before attempting any techniques outlined in this book.

By reading this document, the reader agrees that under no circumstances is the author responsible for any losses, direct or indirect, that are incurred as a result of the use of the information contained within this document, including, but not limited to, errors, omissions, or inaccuracies.

Table of Contents

Introduction 1

Chapter 1: Introduction to Violins 4

Chapter 2: Getting Started with the Violin 15

Chapter 3: Violin Playing Techniques 28

Chapter 4: Building Violin Skills 40

Chapter 5: Playing Violin Music 51

Chapter 6: Violin Care and Maintenance 62

Chapter 7: Exploring Violin History
and Repertoire... 69

Conclusion 80

References 82

Introduction

Have You Ever Heard a Violin Sing?

Close your eyes for a moment. Imagine a sound so beautiful it makes you shiver. A sound that dances and twirls, filling the room with joy and maybe even a tear or two. That, dear friend, is the magic of the violin.

This amazing instrument has been around for centuries, and famous musicians use it to create music that tells stories without words. Now, it's your turn to unlock the secrets of the violin and turn your dreams into reality.

However, you might say, "Isn't learning the violin hard? I don't want to spend hours getting frustrated!"

Well, what if there was a book that made learning the violin easy, fun, and exciting? A book packed with clear instructions, amazing pictures, and amazing stories about violins throughout history?

That's exactly what Violin for Kids is all about.

This book is different. It's not filled with boring black-and-white notes and confusing words. Violin for Kids speaks your language, with pictures that show you exactly what to do and step-by-step instructions so clear you'll be amazed at how quickly you learn.

Here's a sneak peek at the incredible things you'll discover inside:

- **The Violin's Secrets Revealed:** Violin for Kids takes you on a tour of the violin's parts, explaining how each piece works together to make magic happen.

- **Become a Violin Buddy:** Learning to hold the violin properly is tricky, but don't worry. Violin for Kids shows you exactly how to hold your new friend comfortably and confidently so you can focus on making music without feeling awkward.

- **Unlock the Power of the Bow:** The bow is a magic wand for your violin. In this book, you'll learn how to use the bow to create different sounds, from soft hums to powerful shouts. Get ready to amaze your friends and family with your skills.

- **Practice Makes Perfect (But It Doesn't Have to Be Boring):** Learning an instrument can be fun, but sometimes practice feels like a chore. Violin for Kids shows you how to make practicing enjoyable with interesting exercises and tips that will help you improve without even realizing it.

- **Play the Music You Love:** Who says beginners can't play real music? Violin for Kids teaches you how to read music step-by-step so you can start playing simple yet beautiful songs that will have you tapping your toes and wanting more.

- **Unravel the History of Violins:** Did you know violins have been around for hundreds of years? Violin for Kids takes you on a fascinating journey through time, meeting famous composers and learning about the amazing music written for the violin.

- **Keep Your Violin Happy:** Like any friend, your violin needs to be taken care of. This book teaches you how to clean and store your instrument properly so it can continue to create magical music with you for years.

Violin for Kids is filled with everything you need to know to start your musical journey on the right foot. So, are you ready to unlock the magic of the violin and create your beautiful music? Turn the page and get started.

Chapter 1: Introduction to Violins

Have you ever wondered how a simple wooden box creates such beautiful music? Well, wonder no more. In this chapter, you'll be introduced to the amazing tidbits of violins, a member of the string family known for its sweet, soaring melodies.

Prepare to explore the violin's secrets, from the surprising materials it's made of to the fascinating way it produces sound. You'll meet the violin's close relatives (the viola, cello, and double bass) and discover how they all work together to create a symphony of sound.

1. Explore the violin's secrets. Source: https://www.pexels.com/photo/brown-violin-leaning-on-brown-wooden-cabinet-462447/

You'll also discover why learning the violin is an incredible adventure. Get ready to express yourself through music, build confidence with every note you play, and develop a lifelong connection with this magical instrument. Grab your curiosity and set off on your violin journey.

Overview of the Violin as a String Instrument

The violin, the star of today's show, belongs to a special group of instruments called the string family. What makes it stand out from the crowd? It's time to explore the violin's unique look, surprisingly interesting build, and the magic behind its beautiful sound.

The Violin's Dazzling Look

Violins are known for their elegant hourglass shape and come in various sizes to fit different players. Regardless of the size, they all share features that contribute to their beauty and function. Here's a closer look.

- **The Classic Silhouette:** The violin is crafted with a beautiful, curved top made of spruce and a flat back usually made of maple. Did you know that the wood for the violin's top is chosen very carefully? Spruce is preferred because it's light and vibrates easily, which is key to creating a bright, singing sound.

- **Shiny and Smooth:** The violin's body is polished to a smooth finish, making it gleam under the stage lights. Some violins are even adorned with beautiful varnish in different colors, making them true works of art.

- **Four Sparkling Strings:** Violins have four strings, usually made of steel or synthetic materials. These strings stretch from the top of the instrument, where they're securely fastened to tuning pegs, all the way down to the tailpiece at the other end. By turning the tuning pegs, you can adjust how tight the strings are, which controls the pitch of the sound they make.

Wood, Strings, and Music

The violin might look simple, but its clever combination of wood and strings creates beautiful music. Here's a peek inside to see what makes this instrument tick.

- **It's Mostly Wood:** Believe it or not, the violin's body is made from different types of wood. Spruce is used for the top, while maple is used for the back and sides because it's strong and helps project the sound. The fingerboard, where you press your fingers to change notes, is made from a dark hardwood called ebony.

- **The Bridge Is Key:** A small bridge made of maple sits on the violin's body. The strings rest on this bridge, transferring their vibrations to the body, which amplifies the sound. The bridge is a tiny conductor, ensuring the vibrations travel where they need to go to create a beautiful sound.

How Does a Violin Make Music?

When you draw the bow across a string, it makes the string vibrate fast. These vibrations travel through the bridge and into the violin's body, making the whole instrument buzz like a beehive. However, there's a little more to it:

- **The Vibrating Symphony:** The top of the violin, made of spruce, vibrates especially well, amplifying the sound and creating the beautiful tone you hear. The more the wood vibrates, the bigger and stronger the sound is.

- **Pitch Perfect:** By pressing your fingers on the strings at different spots, you can change how much they vibrate, creating different pitches of high and low notes. The shorter the vibrating string length, the higher the pitch. This is why pressing your finger closer to the fingerboard (making the vibrating part of the string shorter) creates a higher note. You'll play all sorts of melodies on your violin by learning how to place your fingers correctly.

So, there you have it. The violin might seem like a complex instrument, but it's all about the fascinating way wood and strings work together to create beautiful music.

The Violin Family

The violin might be the star of the show today, but did you know it has a whole family of string instruments? It's time to meet the violin's siblings: the viola, cello, and double bass, and discover what makes each one of them special.

Size Matters

One of the first things you'll notice about the violin family is size. Just like in a human family, there are big brothers and sisters and, of course, the little one (which, in this case, is the violin).

- **The Big Brother -The Cello:** The cello is the tallest member of the violin family, almost as tall as a grown-up. It's held between the legs while you play and has a deep, rich sound like a gentle giant.

2. *The Cello. Source: https://www.pexels.com/photo/a-cello-beside-a-chair-8519628/*

- **The Big Sister -The Viola:** A bit bigger than the violin but smaller than the cello, the viola is like the middle child. It has a warm, mellow sound that often plays the harmony parts in an orchestra, filling out the music with beautiful tones.

*3. The Viola. Source: The Metropolitan Museum of Art, CC0, via Wikimedia Commons.
https://commons.wikimedia.org/wiki/File:Viola_1884_John_C._Harris_DP-19235-001.jpg*

- **The Little One (But Not Less Important) - The Violin:** Your musical star, the violin, is the smallest of the bunch. Don't let its size fool you, though. The violin has a bright, soaring sound that can sing melodies and dance around the other instruments.

4. The Violin. Source: Pianoplonkers, CC BY-SA 3.0 <https://creativecommons.org/licenses/by-sa/3.0>, via Wikimedia Commons.
https://commons.wikimedia.org/wiki/File:German,_maple_Violin.JPG

How Do They Sound Different?

Even though they're all part of the same family, each member of the violin family has a unique voice. Here's how their sounds differ:

- **Deep Bass Lines:** The cello, the biggest instrument, has the lowest and deepest voice. It can play low, rumbling notes that add foundation to the music, much like the bass drum in a rock band.

- **Warm and Melodic:** The viola has a warm, mellow sound that sits in the middle range. It often plays the harmony parts, filling out the music and creating a rich soundscape.
- **High and Soaring:** The violin, the smallest member, has the highest and brightest voice. It can play fast melodies and create all sorts of emotions with its expressive sound.

Together, the violin family creates a beautiful harmony. It's a musical conversation, with each instrument playing its part to create a symphony of sound.

Why Learn the Violin

So, you've learned all about the violin's cool features and its awesome family. However, why should you consider learning this amazing instrument? Well, buckle up because the reasons are as plentiful and exciting as the melodies you'll soon be creating.

Unleash Your Inner Musician

Learning the violin unlocks a world of musical skills within you. Here's how:

- **Hear the Music in Everything:** As you develop your musical skills, you'll start to hear the world differently. Daily sounds like birds chirping or car horns will take on a new musical meaning, inspiring you to create your melodies.
- **Become a Music Maker:** The joy of playing a beautiful song and filling a room with music you created yourself is unparalleled. Learning the violin gives you the power to express yourself creatively and share your emotions through music.

- **Join the Musical Party:** Violins are popular in all sorts of music, from classical orchestras to rock bands and even folk music groups. Learning the violin opens the doors to playing with others and experiencing the magic of creating music together.

Build Confidence and Shine Like a Star

More than about making beautiful music, learning the violin is about building valuable skills that will benefit you in many ways:

- **Practice Makes Progress:** As you learn new methods and master challenging pieces, you'll experience the satisfaction of accomplishment and a growing sense of confidence in your abilities.

- **Discipline Is Your Superpower:** Learning an instrument takes dedication and practice. By sticking with it, you'll develop discipline, a valuable skill that will help you succeed in all areas of life.

- **Stage Presence Like a Pro:** Performing in front of others is nerve-wracking at first, but as you gain experience playing the violin, you'll learn to overcome stage fright and project confidence, making you a natural in any situation.

Express Yourself in a Whole New Way

The violin is a fantastic tool for creative expression:

- **A Range of Emotions:** The violin can sing a thousand emotions, such as joy, sadness, anger, and love, all through the magic of music. Learning to play allows you to express your feelings uniquely and powerfully.

- **Tell Your Story without Words:** Music is a universal language that touches hearts and connects people across cultures. With the violin, you can create stories and share your unique perspective with the world.
- **A Lifetime of Creativity:** Learning the violin is a journey that will last a lifetime. As you progress, you'll discover new ways to express yourself and explore different musical styles, keeping your creativity flowing for years to come.

By now, you've probably got a pretty good idea of why violins are so cool, right? From their unique construction to their rich history, these instruments are bursting with fascinating details. In the next chapter, you'll take things one step further and get started with your very own violin. You'll discover how to hold it comfortably, get familiar with the bow, and make your first magical sounds. Are you ready to turn your dreams of playing the violin into reality?

Chapter 2: Getting Started with the Violin

You walk into a music store and find a library of shiny instruments waiting just for you. Violins of all sizes line the walls, each one promising beautiful melodies. However, with so many choices, how do you find the perfect violin to become your musical partner? This chapter is your first step to unlocking the secrets of getting started with your violin.

5. *Pick the right violin for you! Source: https://www.pexels.com/photo/a-girl-playing-a-violin-8471824/*

In this chapter, you'll blast off into the violin world, where you'll uncover everything from picking the perfect violin to meeting all its amazing parts, so you'll be ready to make your first musical discoveries. Prepare to transform from a curious explorer to a confident violin owner, ready to make your first magical sounds.

Selecting the Right Violin and Equipment

You're excited to start your violin journey, but before diving headfirst into a sea of melodies, you have to find the perfect violin. Violins aren't one-size-fits-all. They come in a range of sizes to accommodate growing musicians like yourself. Here's how to find the perfect violin size for you:

Size Matters

Violins come in different sizes to fit players of all ages and heights. Just like clothes, a violin that's too big or too small will be uncomfortable to play and might hinder your progress. The right-sized violin will feel like an extension of your arm, allowing you to move your fingers freely and play comfortably.

- **Matching Your Size:** The best way to find the right-sized violin is to visit a reputable violin shop. There, experienced staff will help you measure your arm and match you with the perfect violin size. It's the magic key that unlocks the skill of violin playing.

- **Size Chart Secrets:** Here's a handy size chart to give you a general idea:

Age	Approximate	Violin Size

	Arm Length	
4-6 years old	Less than 16 inches	1/16 or 1/10 size
6-7 years old	16-17 inches	1/8 size
7-8 years old	17-19 inches	1/4 size
8-10 years old	19-20.5 inches	1/2 size
10-12 years old	20.5-22 inches	3/4 size
12+ years old	Over 22 inches	4/4 size (full size)

Essential Equipment

Now that you have your perfect violin, it's time to gather some essential equipment to get you started. Here's your violin starter pack:

- **The Bow Is Your Partner:** The bow makes the strings vibrate and create sound. It's the magic wand that unlocks the violin's voice. Look for a bow made of good-quality wood and with comfortable hair. Quality matters, even for beginners, because a well-made bow will help you produce better sound and make learning more enjoyable.

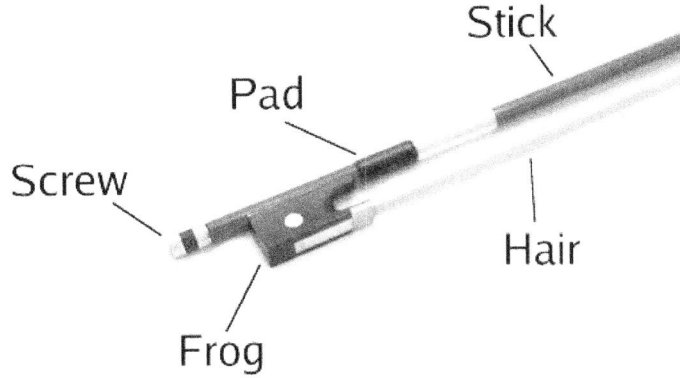

6. The Bow. Source: Kbh3rd, CC BY-SA 3.0 <http://creativecommons.org/licenses/by-sa/3.0/>, via Wikimedia Commons.
https://commons.wikimedia.org/wiki/File:Violin_bow_parts.jpg

- **Rosin Makes the Music Flow:** Rosin is a sticky substance that helps the bow grip the strings and create sound. It adds smoothness to your bow. However, don't overdo it because a little rosin goes a long way.

- **A Shoulder Rest for Comfort:** A shoulder rest helps hold the violin comfortably on your shoulder while you play. It comes in different shapes and sizes, so you can find one that fits you perfectly. Having a good shoulder rest will prevent neck and shoulder aches, especially during longer practice sessions.

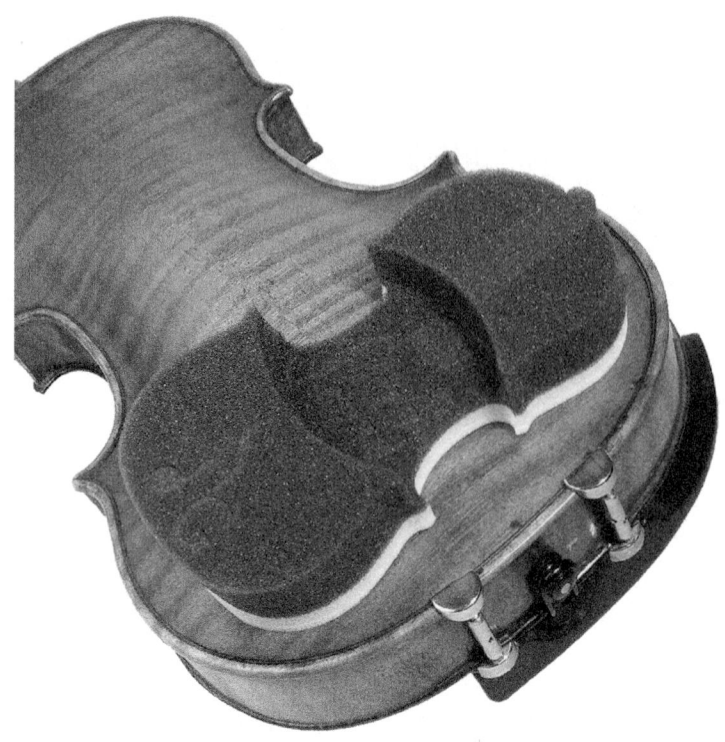

*7. Shoulder rest. Source: Smygfet, CC BY-SA 4.0 <https://creativecommons.org/licenses/by-sa/4.0>, via Wikimedia Commons.
https://commons.wikimedia.org/wiki/File:AcoustaGrip_Soloist.jpg*

- **A Case for Protection:** Your violin is a precious instrument, so it needs a good home. A sturdy case will protect your violin from bumps and scratches while you're on the go. Look for a case that's lightweight yet strong, with enough compartments to hold your violin, bow, rosin, and any sheet music you might need.

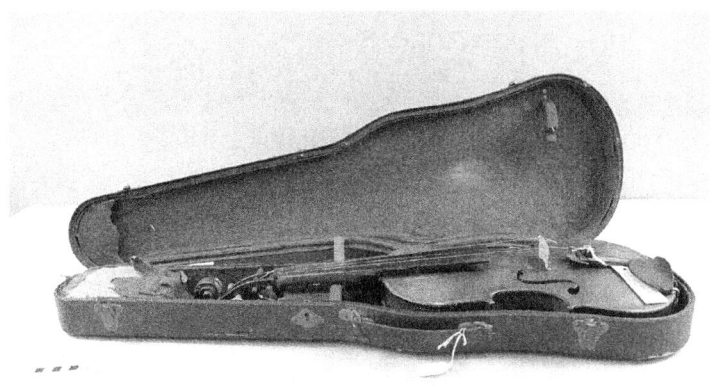

8. *Violin case. Source: Auckland Museum, CC BY 4.0 <https://creativecommons.org/licenses/by/4.0>, via Wikimedia Commons. https://commons.wikimedia.org/wiki/File:Violin_(AM_1998.60.36 3-32).jpg*

Ready to Shop?

Now, you're equipped with the knowledge to find the perfect violin and essential gear. Visiting a reputable violin shop allows you to try different instruments and find one that feels comfortable and sounds beautiful to you. Most shops offer rentals, too, which is a great option for beginners who are still growing. Don't be shy to ask questions. The staff at the violin shop are there to help you find the perfect instrument to kickstart your musical adventure.

Understanding the Basic Parts of the Violin

Congratulations on finding your perfect violin. Now, it's time to know all its amazing parts. Your violin is a musical map, and these parts are the landmarks that will guide you on your playing journey.

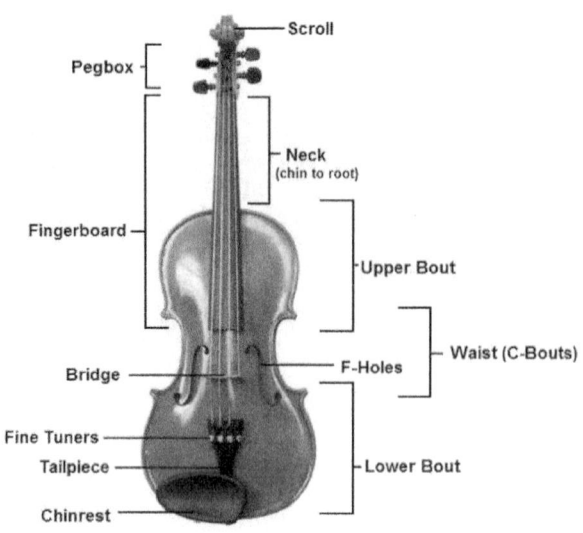

9. Violin parts. Source: Sotakeit, CC BY-SA 3.0 <http://creativecommons.org/licenses/by-sa/3.0/>, via Wikimedia Commons. https://commons.wikimedia.org/wiki/File:Violinconsruction3.JPG

The Fingerboard

The fingerboard is the long, dark piece of wood at the neck of the violin. It's where your fingers press down on the strings to create different notes. Here's a closer look:

- **Smooth and Dark:** The fingerboard is usually made of ebony, a dark and smooth hardwood. This smooth surface allows your fingers to slide easily up and down the neck as you play.

- **Lines and Markers:** Look closely, and you'll see thin black lines and sometimes even dots on the fingerboard. These lines and markers help you position your fingers in the right spots to play different notes.

- **Making Music with Your Fingers:** By pressing down on the strings at different positions on the fingerboard, you change how fast they vibrate, creating different pitches. The closer you press your finger to the bridge (the little stand holding the strings up), the higher the note you'll play.

The Strings

The strings are the heart of the violin's sound, vibrating to create beautiful music. Are you ready to meet them?

- **Four Is the Magic Number:** Violins have four strings, each tuned to a different pitch. From thinnest to thickest (and lowest to highest pitch), they are the E string, A string, D string, and G string. Remember these names by using a handy memory trick: "Every Awesome Dog Gets Sausages."

10. The Violin's strings. Source: Providence Doucet providence, CC0, via Wikimedia Commons. https://commons.wikimedia.org/wiki/File:Violin_strings_in_close -up_(Unsplash).jpg

- **Tuning Up for Fun:** The tuning pegs at the top of the violin control the tightness of the strings. By turning the pegs, you can adjust the pitch of each string, making sure your violin sounds its best.

- **Vibrating with Emotion:** When you draw the bow across a string, it makes the string vibrate fast. These vibrations travel through the body of the violin, creating sound. The tighter the string, the higher the pitch it will vibrate at.

The Top and Back Plates

The violin's body is a beautifully crafted box, and its top and back plates are the two most important parts.

- **The Soundboard:** The top plate, also called the belly or soundboard, is the heart of the violin's sound production. The vibrations from it are what create the violin's beautiful sound. The soundboard is carved with a specific arch that optimizes the sound quality.

- **The Back Plate:** The back plate, also called the back, plays an important role in projecting the sound produced by the top plate. It also resonates and amplifies the sound waves traveling through the violin's body.

- **Keeping It Strong:** The top and back plates are joined together by the ribs, which are thin strips of wood that bend around the sides of the violin. The ribs provide strength and structure to the instrument while also allowing the top and back plates to vibrate freely.

- **Holding the Strings Up High:** The bridge holds the strings off the fingerboard, allowing them to vibrate freely when you play.

- **Transferring the Magic:** When you draw the bow across a string, the vibrations travel down the string and into the bridge. The bridge then transfers these vibrations to the body of the violin, making the whole instrument sing.

The Sound Post

Inside the violin, hidden beneath the bridge, there's a little secret weapon called the sound post. It's a small wooden dowel that supports the top of the violin and transmits the vibrations from the bridge to the back of the instrument. Here's why it's important:

- **It Improves Sound Quality:** The sound post plays a vital role in amplifying the violin's sound and giving it its unique richness and tone. It's a pillar holding the top and back of the violin together in a specific way that optimizes the sound waves traveling through the instrument.

- **Precise Placement:** The placement of the sound post is very important and requires a skilled luthier (violin maker or repairer) to position it correctly. A well-placed sound post will dramatically improve the sound quality of the violin.

- **Delicate Balance:** The sound post is a delicate part of the violin and should not be adjusted by untrained hands. If you think your sound post needs adjustment, take your violin to a qualified luthier.

The Tailpiece

At the opposite end of the violin from the fingerboard sits the tailpiece. This is a thin piece of wood or metal that holds the other ends of the strings securely in place.

- **String Anchors:** The tailpiece has a hole for each string, where a special fastener called a fine tuner is attached. These fine tuners allow you to make small adjustments to the pitch of each string after you've tuned them with the tuning pegs at the top.

- **Keeping it Steady:** The tailpiece also connects to the chinrest with a thin string called the tailgut. This keeps the tailpiece in place and ensures the strings maintain the correct tension.

The Pegbox

The pegbox, a beautifully carved wooden enclosure, sits at the top of the violin's neck. This is where the strings begin and where the tuning pegs are located.

- **Tuning Pegs:** The tuning pegs are similar to the knobs on a radio. By turning them, you can adjust the tightness of each string, which controls the pitch of the sound it makes. Each string has its tuning peg, and they're arranged from the thinnest string (E) to the thickest string (G) as you move from right to left (or vice versa, depending on how you hold the violin).

- **Keeping It Tight:** The pegs are tapered, which means they get thicker at the bottom and thinner at the top. This allows them to be inserted tightly into the pegbox holes and hold the strings securely in place, even with the constant tension pulling from the other end.

The Scroll

The scroll is the beautifully carved decoration at the top of the violin's neck. It's often likened to a curled piece of parchment, and some scrolls are even adorned with intricate designs or animal heads. However, the scroll isn't just there for looks.

- **Balance and Strength:** The scroll plays a role in the violin's balance and strength. It distributes the tension of the strings from the pegbox down the neck of the violin.

- **A Touch of History:** The scroll design has evolved, but it has always been a part of the violin's form. Some believe that the scroll's shape is based on the head of a snail or a mythical creature. Whatever its inspiration, the scroll adds a touch of elegance and history to this beautiful instrument.

The Chinrest

The chinrest is a curved piece of wood or plastic that attaches to the side of the violin's body. As the name suggests, this is where you rest your chin while you play.

- **Comfort Is Key:** A well-fitting chinrest is essential for comfortable playing. It helps you hold the violin securely in place without causing any strain on your neck or jaw. Chinrests come in different shapes and sizes, so you can find one that fits your facial features and playing style perfectly.

- **Not Just for Chins:** While the chinrest provides a comfortable spot for your chin to rest, it also helps to position the violin correctly on your shoulder. This proper positioning is important for good posture and style as you learn to play.

Many violins don't come with a chinrest pre-installed, so you may need to purchase one separately. Violin shops will help you find the right chinrest for your violin and your comfort level.

By now, you've probably got a pretty good idea of what makes a violin tick, and you're ready to pick out your very own partner in musical crime. Once you've chosen your perfect partner and understand its anatomy, it's time to take the next step in your musical adventure.

In the next chapter, you'll learn how to hold your violin comfortably and master the art of the bow. You'll explore different methods and positions to create your first beautiful sounds. Prepare to transform your violin from a cool-looking object into a magical instrument that sings your song.

Chapter 3: Violin Playing Techniques

A sculptor needs to understand the tools before shaping the clay. Similarly, a violinist must master proper posture and hand positioning to translate musical ideas into sound. This chapter is your backstage pass to violin techniques. You'll explore how to hold the violin just right, where to put your fingers to make different sounds, and how to use the bow to make your violin sing loud or soft, high, or low. By the end of this chapter, you'll be ready to start creating beautiful violin melodies.

11. Learn how to hold the violin just right. Source: https://www.pexels.com/photo/a-girl-playing-violin-18752168/

Proper Hand Positioning and Posture

With proper posture and hand position, you'll feel comfortable, avoid injuries, and be well on your way to mastering this amazing instrument. Here are some tips to help you get into your musical hero pose:

Standing Tall

- **Feet First:** Stand comfortably with your feet about shoulder-width apart. Stand tall and proud, ready to conquer the world (or at least the violin).

- **Finding Your Center:** Shift your weight slightly onto the balls of your feet. This will help you maintain good balance and allow you to move your arms and body freely as you play.

- **Spine Straight Up:** Keep your back straight and avoid slouching. Imagine a long string running from the top of your head down your spine, pulling you upward. This will help maintain good posture and prevent back pain.

Finding the Perfect Spot

- **Shoulder Support:** Hold the violin gently between your collarbone and the left side of your jaw. The weight of the violin should be supported primarily by your collarbone, not your arm.

12. *Position your violin between your collarbone and your jaw. Source: https://www.pexels.com/photo/man-person-people-woman-6671607/*

- **Left Hand in Charge:** Your left hand will be on the fingerboard, fingering the strings to create different notes. Your right hand will hold the bow and draw it across the strings to make them vibrate.

Reaching for the Notes with your Left Hand

- **Thumb on Guard:** Your left thumb should be curved gently and placed along the back of the violin's neck, on the opposite side of the fingerboard from your fingers. It should not squeeze the neck or stick out too much. Let your thumb gently hold the violin in place, not gripping it tightly.

- **Fingers Poised and Ready:** Your fingers should be curved and relaxed, resting lightly on the fingerboard. Don't flatten your fingers or tense them up. Let your fingers be little explorers, ready to discover new notes on the violin's map.

Holding the Bow with the Right Hand

- **A Firm but Gentle Grip:** Hold the bow between your thumb and index finger, with the middle finger resting underneath the frog (the part of the bow closest to the grip). The other two fingers can curve gently around the bow without squeezing too tightly.

- **The Right Arm Angle:** Your right arm should be bent at a comfortable elbow angle, with the wrist relaxed. The bow should be roughly parallel to the strings.

Exercises for Good Form

- **Mirror, Mirror on the Wall:** Stand in front of a mirror and practice holding the violin. This will help you ensure your posture is straight and your violin is positioned correctly.

- **The Shoulder Rest Shuffle:** Sit down and hold the violin in a playing position. With your left hand gently resting on the fingerboard, slowly slide the violin up and down your shoulder a few times. This will help you find the sweet spot where the violin feels comfortable and secure.

- **The Relaxed Arm Raise:** Hold the bow in your right hand and extend your arm straight out in front of you. Keep your arm relaxed, and slowly raise it up and down a few times. This will help you loosen up your right arm and shoulder for smooth bowing.

It takes time and practice to develop good posture and hand position. Don't get discouraged if it doesn't feel perfect right away. The key is to be patient, keep practicing these exercises, and focus on feeling comfortable and relaxed while holding the violin.

Bowing and Fingering Basics

The violin, with its soaring melodies and rich tones, is a captivating instrument. However, you must understand the basics before you go on your musical journey. This section will guide you through the two cornerstones of violin playing, which include bowing methods and finger placement.

Bowing Basics

The bow, a vital extension of your arm, is responsible for producing sound on the strings. Here are the two most fundamental strokes:

- **Down Bow (Downstroke):** Draw the bow across the strings, starting at the tip and moving toward the frog (the end opposite the tip). The bow should be slightly angled toward the bridge (the elevated piece where the strings rest). Your right arm should move naturally from the shoulder, with a relaxed wrist.

- **Up Bow (Upstroke):** This is essentially the opposite of the downstroke. The bow starts near the frog and travels toward the tip. Maintain a similar angle and relaxed posture.

Practice these strokes slowly on an open string (a string played without fingering). Focus on achieving a smooth, continuous sound. You can use a metronome or practice along with a slow drone (a sustained note) to develop a steady bow stroke.

Finding Your Notes

After you're comfortable with the bow, explore finger placement on the fingerboard (the black ebony plate where you press down the strings). Focus on the first three notes a violinist learns:

1. **Open E String:** This is the highest-pitched string, played without fingering. It's a great starting point to get a feel for the instrument.

2. **A String – First Finger:** Gently place your first finger on the A string, just behind the first black fret (the raised line across the fingerboard). Press down firmly with the fingertip, ensuring clean contact with the string. Play this note with a down bow or up bow, focusing on producing a clear sound.

3. **E String – Third Finger:** Similar to the A string, place your third finger on the E string, just behind the second black fret. Maintain a firm but relaxed fingertip press.

Practice switching between these three notes using both down and up bows. It takes time and patience to develop clean finger placement, so be gentle with yourself and celebrate each note you sound clearly.

Bonus Tip: As you practice, pay attention to your posture. Sit up straight with the violin comfortably balanced on your shoulder and collarbone. This posture will improve your playing ability and prevent strain.

Bowing Beyond the Basics

Now that you've mastered holding the violin and bow comfortably, it's time to explore how to control the bow to create different sounds and learn some fancy bowing tricks. However, first, ensure your violin is perfectly tuned and ready to sing.

Tuning Up

Can a singer sing a song if the notes are all jumbled up? That's what happens to a violin if it's out of tune. Here's how to make sure your violin sounds its best:

- **The Tuning Fork:** A tuning fork is a metal tool that vibrates at a specific pitch when struck. You'll typically use one tuned to note A (440 Hz).

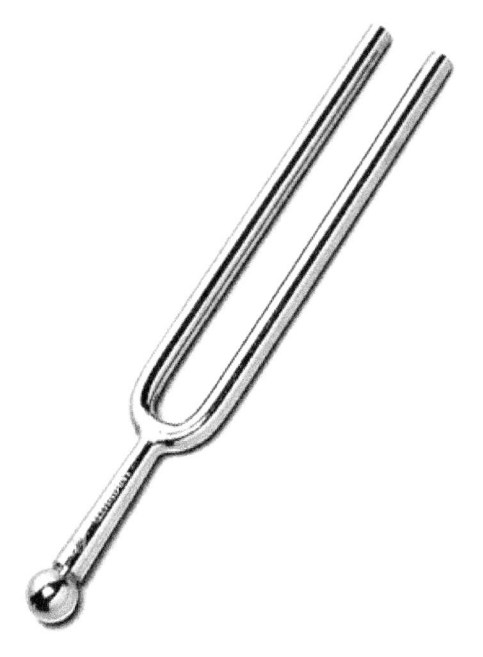

13. The Tuning Fork. Source: Helihark, CC BY-SA 3.0 <https://creativecommons.org/licenses/by-sa/3.0>, via Wikimedia Commons. https://commons.wikimedia.org/wiki/File:Tuning-fork.jpg

- **Matching the Pitch:** Gently tap the tuning fork on a hard surface and place the base of the tuning fork on the top of the violin near the bridge. Pluck the open A string (the thinnest string) on your violin and listen carefully.

- **Turning the Tune:** Use the tuning peg for the A string at the top of the violin's neck. Turn the peg slowly while plucking the string – turning the peg clockwise will tighten the string and raise the pitch, while turning it counter-clockwise will loosen the string and lower the pitch. Adjust the peg until the pitch of your violin's A string matches the vibrating sound of the tuning fork.

- **Tuning the Crew:** Once you've tuned the A string, you can use it as a reference to tune the other strings. Here's the trick: the E string (the second thinnest string) is one whole step higher than the A string, so pluck the open E string and adjust its tuning peg until it sounds pleasant and harmonious with the tuned A string. You can find online resources or violin tuner apps that will guide you through tuning all four strings based on the reference of your tuned A string.

Taking Your Bowing Up a Notch

Before you jump into fancy styles, practice the basic bowing method you learned earlier. Remember, the bow hand should be relaxed, with the wrist curved and the bow roughly parallel to the strings. Draw the bow across the strings, applying gentle pressure to create sound. Here are some exciting new bowing methods to add expression and emotion to your playing:

- **Détaché (Detached):** In detachè bowing, each bow stroke is separate and distinct. You'll see a space between each bow movement as you play.

This is a great way to practice clean notes and get a feel for the bow.

- **Legato (Smooth):** In legato bowing, the bow strokes are connected. There are no gaps between the up and down strokes, creating a smooth and flowing sound. Slur the notes together like singing a beautiful melody.

- **Staccato (Short and Detached):** Staccato bowing creates short and bouncy notes. The bow bounces off the string with each stroke, creating a light and playful sound.

- **Pizzicato (Plucking):** In pizzicato, you pluck the strings with your fingers instead of using the bow. This creates a sharp and percussive sound, adding a surprising element to your playing. You have to pluck the strings like guitar strings.

Practice Makes Perfect

Learning new bowing methods takes time and practice. Don't get discouraged if it feels awkward at first. Here are some tips to help you improve your bowing skills:

- **Start Slow:** Begin by practicing each new method slowly and deliberately. Focus on making clean and controlled bow strokes. As you gain confidence, you can gradually increase your speed.

- **Use a Metronome:** A metronome is a device that clicks at a steady tempo. This can help you practice your bowing with consistent rhythm and timing.

- **Record Yourself:** Record yourself playing and listen back. This can help you identify areas where you can improve your bowing methods.

By consistently practicing these bowing methods, you'll be well on your way to creating beautiful and expressive music on your violin.

Developing a Sense of Pitch and Tone

So far, you've learned how to hold the violin, use the bow, and even tune your instrument. However, to become a true musician, you need to develop a sense of pitch and a beautiful tone. Don't worry; these skills can be learned and improved with a little practice and some fun exercises.

Pitch Perfect: Hitting the Right Notes

If a singer keeps singing slightly sharp or flat, it wouldn't sound very pleasant, would it? The same goes for the violin. A good sense of pitch allows you to play notes accurately and in tune. Here are some tips to help you develop your inner pitch master:

- **Sing It First:** Before you play a note on the violin, try singing it out loud first. This will help connect the sound of the note with your ear.

- **The Tuning Fork Trick:** Remember your trusty tuning fork? Use it to play reference notes like A or E. Try matching the pitch of your violin's open strings to the tuning fork's sound. This will train your ear to recognize the correct pitch.

- **Listen Up:** Pay close attention to the music you hear around you, whether it's on the radio, in a movie, or even sung by a friend. Try to identify the different pitches and melodies you hear. The more you listen, the better your ear will become at recognizing and distinguishing pitches.

Tone Time

The tone of your violin is its voice. It's the quality of the sound it produces. A beautiful tone is rich, warm, and pleasant to listen to. Here's how to develop your tone-producing skills:

- **Bow Control Is Key:** Using gentle pressure with the bow is crucial for creating a good tone. Experiment with applying different amounts of pressure as you draw the bow across the strings. Too little pressure will result in a weak sound, while too much pressure will create a scratchy or harsh tone.

- **Slow and Steady Wins the Race:** Don't rush. Take your time practicing bowing methods and focus on creating a smooth and even sound. As you gain control and confidence with the bow, you'll naturally develop a better tone.

- **Listen to the Masters:** Listen to recordings of professional violinists. Pay attention to the quality and beauty of their sound. As you practice, try to emulate their bowing methods and tone production.

Fun Ear Training Exercises

Learning shouldn't feel like a chore. Here are some engaging exercises to develop your sense of pitch and tone:

- **The Matching Game:** Ask a friend or family member to play a simple melody on a piano or sing a few notes. Try to play the same melody back on your violin, matching the pitches you heard.

- **The Mystery Note Game:** Have someone play a single note on the piano or another instrument while blindfolded. Can you guess the correct note on your violin?

- **Sing and Play:** Find recordings of simple melodies online or in children's songbooks. Try singing along with the recording while playing the melody on your violin. This is a great way to practice matching pitch and developing coordination between your ears and your playing.

By consistently practicing these exercises and focusing on listening and control, you'll develop a keen sense of pitch and a beautiful, warm tone on your violin.

Having mastered the basics covered in this chapter, you've laid a strong foundation for your violin journey. You've learned the basics of proper hand position, mastered some essential bow strokes, and discovered the power of finger placement. Now, you have the tools to turn any simple melody into a masterpiece.

As you move forward, these methods will become second nature, freeing you to focus on expressing yourself through music. Keep practicing, keep exploring, and experiment with different sounds. Grab your violin, let your creativity flow, and amaze everyone with your newfound skills.

Chapter 4: Building Violin Skills

Remember all the awesome tricks you learned in the last chapter? You're a master of holding your violin, a finger placement pro, and a bow-wielding champion. Now, it's time to take your skills to the next level and unlock the secrets of making real music. This chapter is packed with fun exercises to help you practice your bowing methods and finger placement for simple melodies. You'll also crack the code of violin sheet music, a secret map that tells you exactly what to play. By the end of this chapter, you'll be reading music and playing melodies like a boss.

14. *Get ready to read the music sheet like a professional! Source: https://www.pexels.com/photo/a-diligent-girl-playing-violin-8471931/*

Playing Your First Melodies

Congratulations. You've mastered the basics of holding your violin, using the bow, and even training your ear. Now comes the most exciting part. It's time to start creating your music. Get ready to bring the strings to life and play your first melodies.

Mastering the Bow

Before you dive into melodies, take some time to revisit the basic bowing methods you learned:

- **Détaché Review:** This is where each bow stroke is separate and clear, like little hops across the strings. Practice playing long, slow bows on a single string, focusing on making clean and even sounds. Play as if you're bouncing a small ball on the string with each stroke of the bow.

- **Legato Challenge:** Time to connect the bows. In legato bowing, the bow strokes are smooth and flowing, creating a singing sound. Practice slowly at first, making sure there are no gaps between your up and down bow strokes. Try slurring the notes together like silky-smooth melted chocolate.

Placing Your Fingers on the Fingerboard

Once your bowing is in tip-top shape, prepare to explore finger placement on the fingerboard. The frets are guidelines for where to put your fingers to create different notes.

- **Open Strings:** The simplest notes to play are the open strings, which you don't press down with your fingers. Try plucking each string one at a time (pizzicato) and listening to the different pitches they create.

- **First Finger:** Add one finger to the mix. Gently place the first finger of your left hand on the string closest to you (the E string), right between the first and second frets. This will create a new note that sounds higher than the open E string. Play this new note with a detaché bow stroke, then pluck the open E string right after. Can you hear the difference in pitch? Let your finger add a new word to the string's song.

Putting It All Together

You're ready to play your first melody. Here's a super simple song called "Hot Cross Buns" that uses only the open E string and the first finger on the E string (between the first and second frets):

Hot cross buns, hot cross buns,

One a penny, two a penny,

Hot cross buns.

Play the open E string for "Hot," then put your first finger down for "cross." Keep alternating between the open string and the first finger for the rest of the song. Play each note with a detaché bow stroke. Slow and steady wins the race.

Fun Exercises to Level Up

As you continue your violin journey, here are some ways to keep things fun and engaging:

- **Challenge Time:** Once you've mastered "Hot Cross Buns," try playing the melody on the A string (the next string over) instead of the E string. Adjust your finger placement. Your first finger will now go between the second and third frets on the A string. Let your finger press a new button on the fingerboard, creating a different sound.

- **Duet Play:** Grab a friend or family member and play "Hot Cross Buns" together. One person can play the melody on the E string, while the other plays it on the A string. You can create a mini violin orchestra in your own home.

- **Composing:** Feeling creative? Try making up your short melody by using the open E string and the first finger on the E string. Can you play your creation with a detaché or legato bow? Look at yourself as a composer, writing your special song for the violin.

- **Sticker Success:** As you learn new notes and songs, reward yourself with a fun sticker chart. Every time you master a new skill, add a sticker.

Seeing a chart filled with stickers is a great way to track your progress and celebrate your achievements.

Have fun and enjoy the learning process. Celebrate your small victories, keep practicing, and don't be afraid to experiment. The violin awaits your musical adventures. There's a whole world of beautiful melodies waiting for you to play.

Understanding Violin Sheet Music

You've been making amazing progress on your violin. Now, it's time to learn how to read violin sheet music, a secret code that tells you what notes to play and when to play them. With a little practice, you'll be decoding music in no time and playing your favorite songs on the violin.

The Staff

As you begin reading violin sheet music, you'll find five lines and four spaces in between. This is called the staff, and it's the foundation for writing musical notes. The lines and spaces each represent different pitches similar to the frets on your violin fingerboard.

- **Treble Clef:** At the beginning of the staff, you'll see a symbol that looks a little like a fancy G. This is called the treble clef, and it tells you that the staff is designed specifically for higher-pitched instruments like the violin.

Treble Clef

Now that you know the staff, it's time to meet the musical notes that live on it. Each note is represented by an oval head and a stem. The position of the note on the staff tells you which pitch to play. Here are the first few notes you'll encounter on the violin, all living on the treble clef staff:

- **Treble Clef Lines:** The lines of the staff, going from bottom to top, are named E, G, B, D, and F. These lines are where most of your beginning violin notes will reside.

- **Space Cadets:** The spaces between the lines also have names: F, A, C, and E. These spaces can also hold notes.

Keeping the Beat

More than just about the notes, music is also about rhythm. Rhythm refers to the length of time each note is played. Sheet music uses symbols to tell you how long to hold each note. Here are some basic rhythms you'll see in beginner violin music:

- **Whole Note:** A whole note looks like a filled-in oval and gets you to hold the sound for four beats.

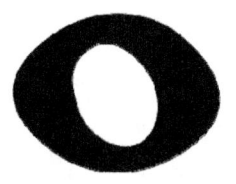

15. Whole Note. Source: Matrix0123456789, Public domain, via Wikimedia Commons.
https://commons.wikimedia.org/wiki/File:Whole_note.svg

- **Half Note:** A half note looks like a filled-in oval with a stem on the right side. It gets you to hold the sound for two beats.

16. Half Note. Source: Adam Arredondo, Public domain, via Wikimedia Commons.
https://commons.wikimedia.org/wiki/File:Half_Note.JPG

- **Quarter Note:** A quarter note looks like a filled-in oval with a stem and a single flag on the right side of the stem. It gets you to hold the sound for one beat.

17. Quarter Note. Source: Adam Arredondo, Public domain, via Wikimedia Commons.
https://commons.wikimedia.org/wiki/File:Quarter_Note.JPG

Interactive Challenge

Why don't you try reading some simple rhythms? See if you can clap or tap your foot along to these rhythms:

- **Whole Note Power:** Clap once and hold for four counts. (This represents one whole note.)
- **Half Note Harmony:** Clap once and hold for two counts, then clap again and hold for two counts. (This represents two half notes.)
- **Quarter Note Quartet:** Clap four times in a steady beat. (This represents four quarter notes.)

Reading Your First Notes

Now that you know the staff, the notes, and some basic rhythms, you're ready to tackle your first piece of sheet music. Here's a super simple melody written on the treble clef staff using just quarter notes:

E E D D C C B B

This little melody uses the open E string, the first finger on the E string (between the first and second frets), and the first finger on the A string (between the second and third frets). Can you play it slowly and steadily on your violin, following the rhythm of the quarter notes?

Keep Exploring

As you progress on your violin journey, you'll learn more about different notes, rhythms, and musical symbols. Don't worry; take it one step at a time. Many resources are available online and in music stores that will help you continue learning how to read sheet music.

The key is to have fun and keep practicing. The more you read and play, the easier it will become to translate the musical symbols into beautiful melodies on your violin.

Conquering Practice Time

By now, you've unlocked some amazing violin skills. You can hold the violin comfortably, use the bow to create different sounds, and even play your first melodies. However, just like any superhero needs regular training, becoming a violin master requires consistent practice. This section will equip you with some powerful practice tips to help you make the most of your violin time.

Setting SMART Goals

Any superhero without a mission wouldn't know where to fly or who to save, would they? Setting goals is your personal practice mission statement. It gives you direction and helps you track your progress. Here's how to set SMART goals for violin practice:

- **Specific:** Instead of saying, "I want to play better," try "I will practice playing détaché bow strokes with clean and even sound for five minutes every day."

- **Measurable:** How will you know you're achieving your goal? Record yourself playing and compare your recordings over time.

- **Attainable:** Don't overwhelm yourself with super difficult goals right away. Start with small, achievable goals and gradually increase the difficulty as you improve.

- **Relevant:** Ensure your goals are relevant to your current skill level and what you want to achieve overall.

- **Time-bound:** Set a realistic timeframe for achieving your goals. For example, you might aim to master a new bowing method by the end of the week.

Taming Practice Time Distractions

Even the best players get distracted sometimes. Here are some tips to help you stay focused during practice:

- **Find Your Practice Zone:** Choose a quiet space with minimal distractions where you can concentrate on your violin. Turn off the TV, put your phone away, and let your family or roommates know you'll be practicing.
- **Break It Down:** Don't try to learn everything at once. Break down your practice session into smaller, manageable chunks. Focus on a specific skill for a few minutes before moving on to the next one.
- **Take Breaks:** You need to recharge with short breaks during your practice session. Get up, stretch, grab a healthy snack, and come back to your violin feeling refreshed and ready to focus again.

Building Your Practice Routine

Every superhero needs a training schedule. A practice routine is your personalized violin training plan. Here are some tips for building a routine that works for you:

- **Start Small:** Begin with shorter practice sessions, like 15 to 20 minutes a day, and gradually increase the duration as you get more comfortable.
- **Consistency Is Key:** It's better to practice for a shorter amount of time every day than to have long,

occasional practice sessions. Aim for daily practice, even if it's just for a short while.

- **Warm-Up and Cool-Down:** Just like athletes, warming up your muscles before playing prevents injuries. Spend a few minutes at the beginning of your practice session doing some gentle stretches and exercises for your fingers and arms. At the end of your practice, do some cool-down stretches to relax your muscles.

- **Make It Fun:** Learning the violin should be enjoyable. Incorporate activities you find fun into your practice routine. Play along with your favorite songs, learn a new melody you love, or challenge yourself with a fun bowing method.

There's no one-size-fits-all practice routine. Experiment and find what works best for you. The most important thing is to be consistent, have fun, and celebrate your progress.

Look at you go. You can now play melodies on your violin, understand what the symbols on the page mean, and practice like a champion. The more you practice, the more songs you'll be able to play. Keep exploring different melodies, keep reading music, and keep up your awesome practice routine. The sky's the limit for your violin skills. You might even compose your own music someday.

Chapter 5: Playing Violin Music

From the fancy classical pieces, you might hear in movies to toe-tapping folk tunes that make you want to dance, there are countless different styles to explore. In this chapter, you'll discover various ways violins create exciting sounds. You'll find some short snippets of famous violin pieces from each style. You'll also learn the secret language of emotions in music. How can you make your violin sound happy, sad, or even spooky? Buckle up and prepare to play music that will make you and everyone around you feel special.

18. Discover various ways violins create exciting sounds. Source: Designed by Freepik. https://www.freepik.com/free-vector/playing-violin-concept-illustration_42107500.htm

A Young Violinist's Guide to Genres

Have you ever imagined your violin soaring through a lively jig, wailing with a blues band, or even rocking out with a heavy metal group? Believe it or not, the violin isn't just for playing fancy classical pieces. This amazing instrument is your passport to a whole world of musical styles, each with its unique sound and story to tell. So, buckle up, young violinist because it's time for an adventure.

Classical

- **Overview:** This is probably where most violinists begin their journey. Classical music features beautiful melodies and complex harmonies, often played by orchestras, chamber groups, or soloists. The music can be dramatic, playful, or anything in between.

- **Famous Artists:** Niccolò Paganini, Wolfgang Amadeus Mozart, Anne Akiko Meyers.

- **Famous Songs:** Violin Concerto in E minor by Mendelssohn, Frühling (Spring) from The Four Seasons by Vivaldi.

- **Practice Tips:** Focus on clean notes, perfect posture, and following the written music carefully. Classical music is a great way to build a strong foundation for all other styles.

19. Niccolò Paganini. Source: http://paganiniccolo.blogspot.it, Public domain, via Wikimedia Commons. https://commons.wikimedia.org/wiki/File:Niccol%C3%B2_Pagani ni_ritratto_giovanile.jpg

Folk and Fiddle

- **Overview:** Folk music is all about storytelling and tradition. Fiddle music is a type of folk music that's full of lively jigs, toe-tapping reels, and heart-wrenching ballads. It often uses improvisation (making up music on the spot.), double stops (playing two notes at once), and drones (a long, continuous note).

- **Famous Artists:** Itzhak Perlman (who also played classical), Ashley MacIsaac, Natalie MacMaster.

- **Famous Songs:** The Orange Blossom Special, Devil Went Down to Georgia, Ashokan Farewell.

- **Practice Tips:** Learn how to play with a strong, steady bow and experiment with double stops and drones. Add your little flourishes and improvisations.

20. Natalie MacMaster. Source: Filberthockey at English Wikipedia, Public domain, via Wikimedia Commons. https://commons.wikimedia.org/wiki/File:Natalie_MacMaster_at_MerleFest,_2004.gif

Bluegrass

- **Overview:** Bluegrass is a high-energy style of music with roots in American folk and mountain music. It features fast picking and intricate melodies and often includes instruments like the banjo, mandolin, and guitar. The violin plays a key role in providing harmony and counterpoint (melodies that complement the main tune).

- **Famous Artists:** Alison Krauss, Johnny Gimble, Stéphane Grappelli.

- **Famous Songs:** Foggy Mountain Breakdown, Orange Blossom Special (yes, it appears in Bluegrass, too.), The Devil Comes Back to Georgia.

- **Practice Tips:** Work on fast, clean picking and try to listen closely to the other instruments in the band to create a tight, blended sound.

21. Stéphane Grappelli. Source: Allan warren, CC BY-SA 3.0 <https://creativecommons.org/licenses/by-sa/3.0>, via Wikimedia Commons.
https://commons.wikimedia.org/wiki/File:Stephane_Grappelli_Allan_Warren.jpg

Rock and Pop

- **Overview:** Who says rock and pop can't have violins? Electric violins and even traditional violins with special effects add a unique twist to your favorite tunes. This genre is all about expressing yourself and having fun with the music.

- **Famous Artists:** Lindsey Stirling, Vanessa Mae, Nigel Kennedy.

- **Famous Songs:** What a Wonderful World by Louis Armstrong (played by Vanessa Mae),

Bohemian Rhapsody by Queen (covered by Lindsey Stirling).

- **Practice Tips:** Experiment with different effects pedals and ways to create unique sounds. Improvise solos and let your inner rockstar shine.

22. Lindsey Stirling. Source: Gage Skidmore from Peoria, AZ, United States of America, CC BY-SA 2.0 <https://creativecommons.org/licenses/by-sa/2.0>, via Wikimedia Commons.
https://commons.wikimedia.org/wiki/File:Lindsey_Stirling_(7486855766).jpg

World Music

- **Overview:** The world is full of amazing musical traditions, and the violin can be found in many of them. From the haunting melodies of Irish fiddling to the dynamic rhythms of Klezmer (Jewish folk music), many different sounds are waiting to be explored.

- **Famous Artists:** Yehudi Menuhin (who played music from all over the world), Lakshminarayana Subramaniam (Indian classical violinist).

- **Famous Songs:** The Butterfly by The Chieftains (Irish fiddle), Hora Staccato (a popular Klezmer piece).
- **Practice Tips:** Listen to music from different cultures and try to find recordings of violins in those styles. Pay attention to the unique rhythms, scales, and ornaments used in each genre.

23. Yehudi Menuhin. Source: Yehudi_Menuhin_&_Stephane_Grappelli_Allan_Warren.jpg: Allan warrenderivative work: Parzi, CC BY-SA 3.0 <https://creativecommons.org/licenses/by-sa/3.0>, via Wikimedia Commons. https://commons.wikimedia.org/wiki/File:Yehudi_Menuhin_1976.jpg

This is just a taste of the incredible variety of music you can play on the violin. The most important thing is to have fun, explore different styles, and find the music that speaks to you.

Methods for Expressive Violin Playing

After you've explored the vast musical landscape of the violin, dive deeper and unlock the secrets of playing with feeling and expression. Your violin is a voice waiting to tell a story. Here are some ways to transform your playing from being technically sound to truly captivating:

Dynamics

When something exciting happens, your voice naturally gets louder, right? Dynamics in music work the same way. They refer to the volume of your playing, allowing you to create dramatic contrasts between whispers and powerful pronouncements.

- **Practice Tip:** Pay close attention to the markings on your sheet music. "p" stands for piano (soft), while "f" stands for forte (loud), and everything in between. Experiment with gradual crescendos (getting louder) and decrescendos (getting softer) to build tension and release in your playing.

Articulation

Articulation refers to how you start and stop your notes. It adds punctuation to your musical sentences. Different articulations create a wide range of moods, from crisp and lively to smooth and legato (connected).

- **Practice Tip:** Learn about different articulations like staccato (short and detached notes), legato (connected notes), and tenuto (held notes). Try playing a simple melody with different articulations and hear how the mood changes.

Bow Control

Your bow is your paintbrush, and the strings are your canvas. By mastering different bowing methods, you can create a rich sound full of emotion.

- **Practice Tip:** Explore methods like spiccato (bouncing the bow on the string for a light, staccato effect) and detache (separate strokes with the bow for a clear, articulated sound). Experiment with different bow speeds and pressures to create a variety of textures in your playing.

Phrasing

Have you noticed a singer taking a breath between phrases for emphasis? Phrasing in music works similarly. It's about grouping notes and playing them with a sense of natural flow and direction. Just like breathing, phrasing helps the music "breathe" and come alive.

- **Practice Tip:** Listen to recordings of great violinists and pay attention to how they phrase the music. Try to identify natural pauses and breathing points in the melody. Practice playing phrases with a connected bow stroke, emphasizing the beginning and end of each phrase.

Dynamics, articulation, bow control, and phrasing all work together to create expressive and emotive violin playing. By mastering these methods, you'll tap into the heart of the music and truly connect with your audience.

You've officially graduated from violin boot camp. You can play melodies, understand music notation, and explore different musical styles. The most amazing thing you've learned is how to use your violin to tell stories. By using dynamics (playing loud or soft) and articulation (how smoothly you connect notes), you'll start expressing all kinds of feelings through your music. The violin becomes your voice, and you can use it to make people laugh, cry, feel happy, or even feel scared.

Chapter 6: Violin Care and Maintenance

Your violin is your partner in musical adventures. Just like any good friend, it needs a little TLC (Tender Loving Care) to keep it happy and healthy. This chapter is all about becoming a violin care champion. You'll learn how to clean and care for your violin properly so it always sounds its best. You'll also discover the best way to store your violin safely and how to handle it with care to avoid any bumps or bruises. Plus, you'll learn how to troubleshoot some common violin problems so you can be a violin fixer and sort out any minor issues that might come up. By the end of this chapter, you'll be a violin care expert, ready to keep your musical buddy in tip-top shape.

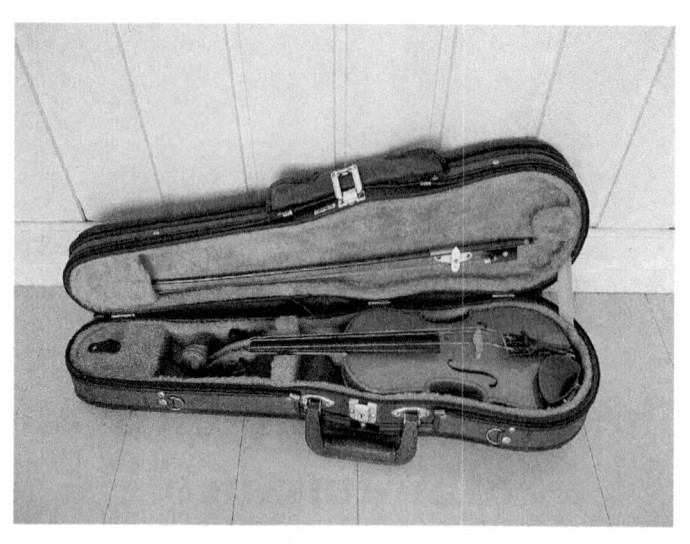

24. *Don't forget to take care of your violin. Source: Santeri Viinamäki, CC BY-SA 4.0 <https://creativecommons.org/licenses/by-sa/4.0>, via Wikimedia Commons. https://commons.wikimedia.org/wiki/File:Violin_in_case_20180808.jpg*

A Guide to Proper Maintenance

Proper care will keep your violin looking its best and ensure it plays smoothly and lasts a lifetime. Here's a quick guide to keeping your violin in top condition:

Cleaning

- **Regular Dusting:** A soft, clean microfiber cloth is your best friend for everyday dusting. Gently wipe down the entire instrument, including the body, fingerboard, strings, and chinrest, to remove rosin dust and fingerprints.

- **Deep Cleaning (optional):** For more thorough cleaning every few months, you can dampen your cloth with a very small amount of distilled water.

Wring it out completely so it's barely damp, and then wipe down the body of the violin gently. Never use any harsh chemicals or polishes on your violin, as they damage the varnish.

Rosin Application

Rosin creates friction between the bow and the strings, allowing you to produce sound.

- **The Right Amount:** Before you start playing, gently draw the bow back and forth across the cake of rosin a few times. You should see a slightly cloudy white trail on the strings.

String Care

Strings are essential for creating sound, and they need to be replaced regularly.

- **Signs for Replacement:** As you play, your strings will eventually lose their brightness and response. Look out for signs like fraying, discoloration, or difficulty holding a tune.

- **Frequency of Change:** How often you need to change your strings depends on how much you play and the climate where you live. Generally, beginners change their strings every few months, while more experienced players change them more frequently.

- **Leave It to the Professionals:** While changing strings is a relatively simple process, it's important to do it correctly to avoid damaging your instrument. If you're a beginner, it's best to take your violin to a qualified luthier (violin maker or repairer) for string changes and other maintenance needs.

By following these simple tips, you can ensure your violin stays in top condition for years to come. A well-maintained violin sounds better and is more enjoyable to play. So, take good care of your musical companion and keep the beautiful melodies flowing.

Storage and Handling Tips

Your violin is a precious instrument, and proper handling and storage are crucial to prevent damage. Here's how to ensure your violin stays safe and ready to play whenever inspiration strikes:

Storage

- **The Case Is King:** Your violin's hard case is its castle. When you're not playing, always store your violin securely inside the case.

- **Location:** Choose a cool, dry place with stable temperature and humidity for your violin's home. Avoid storing it near vents, radiators, or direct sunlight, as extreme temperatures and humidity fluctuations can damage the wood and crack the varnish.

- **Standing Tall:** Inside the case, your violin should rest upright, secured by the plush lining and any included straps or cushions. Never lay it flat in the case, as this puts pressure on the bridge and causes warping.

Handling

- **The Golden Rule:** Always handle your violin with clean, dry hands. Rosin dust, sweat, and oils from your skin damage the varnish over time.

- **Support System:** Get a good grip when holding your violin. Use one hand on the neck (avoiding the fingerboard) and the other hand underneath the body, supporting the scroll (the curled top part) with your thumb.

- **Bow Wow:** Your bow deserves care, too. Loosen the bow hair slightly before storing it in the case. This prevents the hair from becoming stretched or warped. When holding the bow, grip it near the frog (the carved section at the bottom) and avoid touching the delicate hair with your fingers.

These simple storage and handling guidelines will keep your violin safe from harm and ensure it continues to produce beautiful music for years. A little care goes a long way in protecting your musical investment.

Troubleshooting Common Violin Problems

Even the best-cared-for violins experience minor hiccups sometimes. Don't worry, young violinist. Here are some solutions to a few common problems you might encounter:

Broken String

- **Don't Panic:** It happens to everyone. Carefully loosen the tuning peg of the broken string until it has very little tension.

- **Safely Remove:** Using a string cutter (or carefully with pliers), clip the broken string near the bridge and tailpiece. Then, gently unwind the remaining string from the peg box and tailpiece.

- **String Replacement:** This might be a good time to ask a grown-up for help. Replacing a string requires threading it through the peg box and tailpiece and then carefully tuning it to the correct pitch.

25. *Don't forget to replace your strings. Source: Just plain Bill, CC BY-SA 3.0 <http://creativecommons.org/licenses/by-sa/3.0/>, via Wikimedia Commons.*
https://commons.wikimedia.org/wiki/File:Coiled_strings.JPG

Slipping Pegs

- **Tuning Tune-Up:** Sometimes, a slipping peg just needs a little tightening. Ask a grown-up to help with this, as over-tightening will damage the peg. They can use a peg compound (a special paste) to create more friction between the peg and the peg box.

- **Environmental Culprit:** Dry weather makes pegs slip more easily. Consider using a humidifier in your room to maintain proper humidity levels.

Rosin Buildup

- **A Clean Sweep:** If your playing sounds scratchy, it might be because there's too much rosin on the strings. Wipe them down with a clean, soft cloth to remove some of the buildup.
- **Rosin Ritual:** Less is more. Apply rosin to your bow only when needed and in small amounts.

These are just a few basic troubleshooting tips. If you encounter a more complex problem with your violin, it's always best to consult a qualified luthier for assistance. They will diagnose the issue and perform any necessary repairs to keep your violin happy and healthy.

You've officially mastered the art of violin care. You know how to clean it, store it safely, and even troubleshoot any minor problems that might arise. Now, you can be confident that your violin will always be ready to make beautiful music with you. Taking good care of your violin shows how much you appreciate its friendship. The better you treat it, the longer it will last, and the more amazing music you will create together.

Chapter 7: Exploring Violin History and Repertoire

Have you ever wondered where the violin came from or who the coolest violinists of all time were? This chapter is a time machine that will whisk you away on an adventure through the fascinating history of the violin. You'll explore how the violin evolved from its ancient ancestors, meet some legendary violin players who changed the world with their music, and even discover some of the most famous violin pieces ever written.

26. *Explore how the violin evolved from its ancient ancestors. Source: https://www.pexels.com/photo/brown-string-guitar-306175/*

Exploring History and Culture

The violin's journey through time is as dynamic as the music it creates. Buckle up because you're going on a historical adventure.

From Humble Beginnings to Orchestral Star (16th-18th Centuries)

- **The Birth of a Star:** The violin emerged in its modern form around the 16th century in Northern Italy, the land of Stradivari and Amati, legendary violin makers whose instruments are still prized today. These early violins were handcrafted masterpieces known for their warm, mellow sound.

- **From Folk to Fancy:** Initially, violins were played in folk music and dance tunes. However, composers like Monteverdi started incorporating them into orchestral works, forever changing the musical landscape.

Innovation and Evolution (19th-20th Centuries)

- **The Power of Performance:** The 19th century saw the rise of the virtuoso violinist, soloists who dazzled audiences with their technical skill and musicality. This era also saw the development of the modern bow, allowing for greater expressiveness in playing.

- **Beyond the Classics:** The violin wasn't confined to concert halls. Fiddlers in places like America and Ireland kept folk traditions alive, while composers explored new musical styles like jazz and bluegrass, incorporating the violin in unique ways.

A Global Voice (20th Century – Present)

- **World Music Takes Center Stage:** The 20th century witnessed a renewed interest in world music traditions. From the haunting melodies of the Indian violin to the fiery passion of flamenco, the violin became a bridge between cultures.

- **Electric Revolution:** The invention of the electric violin opened up new possibilities. Today, violinists are found rocking out in heavy metal bands or adding a touch of elegance to electronic music.

Interesting Facts

- The names Stradivarius and Amati are not just brands. They're families of luthiers who passed down their violin-making secrets for generations.

- What is the secret to the incredible sound of a Stradivarius violin? It might be the type of wood used and the unique varnish recipe, which is still a mystery today.

- The violin may look delicate, but it's a surprisingly tough instrument. The tension of the strings can withstand over 100 pounds of pressure.

The violin's story is a testament to its versatility and enduring appeal. It's an instrument that has traveled the world, graced countless concert halls, and been a voice for countless cultures. The next time you pick up your violin, remember the rich history it embodies and the endless musical possibilities it holds.

Renowned Violinists and Iconic Compositions

Throughout history, countless violinists have captivated audiences with their artistry. Here are a few legends and some of the most important violin compositions:

The Early Virtuosos (17th-18th Centuries)

- **Arcangelo Corelli (1653-1713):** An Italian violinist and composer, Corelli is considered one of the fathers of violin technique. His concerti grossi (concertos for a large group of instruments) laid the foundation for orchestral music.

- **Antonio Vivaldi (1678-1741):** Another Italian maestro, Vivaldi is best known for his lively violin concertos, including the ever-popular "The Four Seasons." This set of four concertos depicts scenes from each season, bringing nature's beauty to life through music.

- **Johann Sebastian Bach (1685-1750):** The German composer Bach was a master of the organ and harpsichord. He wrote several beautiful pieces for solo violin, showcasing the instrument's range and expressiveness.

27. Arcangelo Corelli. Source: Hugh Howard (1675-1737), Public domain, via Wikimedia Commons. https://commons.wikimedia.org/wiki/File:Arcangelo_Corelli,_portrait_by_Hugh_Howard_(1697)_-_2.jpg

The Romantics and Beyond (19th-20th Centuries)

- **Niccolò Paganini (1782-1840):** This Italian violinist was a rockstar of his time. Renowned for his technical wizardry and showmanship, Paganini pushed the boundaries of what was thought possible on the violin.

- **Pyotr Ilyich Tchaikovsky (1840-1893):** The Russian composer Tchaikovsky wrote one of the most beloved violin concertos ever composed. Full of drama and passion, it's a true showstopper for violinists.

- **Fritz Kreisler (1875-1962):** An Austrian violinist whose career spanned the late 19th and early 20th centuries, Kreisler was known for his sweet tone and expressive playing. He also wrote many beautiful violin pieces himself.

28. Pyotr Ilyich Tchaikovsky. Source: Émile Reutlinger, Public domain, via Wikimedia Commons.
https://commons.wikimedia.org/wiki/File:Tchaikovsky_by_Reutlinger_(cropped).jpg

20th and 21st Century Stars

- **Yehudi Menuhin (1916-1999):** This British violinist championed music from all over the world, not just the classical repertoire. He believed that music could be a force for good in the world.
- **Itzhak Perlman (b. 1945):** An Israeli-American violinist, Perlman is known for his virtuosity and passionate performances. He's also a dedicated advocate for music education.

Bonus: Beyond Classical

- **Stéphane Grappelli (1908-1997):** A French jazz violinist, Grappelli is considered a pioneer of jazz violin. His collaborations with guitarist Django Reinhardt created a unique sound that continues to inspire musicians today.
- **Lindsey Stirling (b. 1986):** An American violinist who incorporates electronic music and dance into her performances, Stirling is a true innovator. Her music shows that the violin can be a powerful voice in any genre.

29. Itzhak Perlman. Source: Kenneth C. Zirkel, CC BY-SA 4.0 <https://creativecommons.org/licenses/by-sa/4.0>, via Wikimedia Commons.
https://commons.wikimedia.org/wiki/File:Itzhak_Perlman_violinist_1984.jpg

This is just a taste of the incredible violinists and compositions out there. With so many styles and eras to explore, musical discovery awaits you.

Innovation and the Evolving Violin

The violin's story is far from over. Just like the instrument itself, the style of violin playing is constantly evolving. Here's a glimpse into some exciting advancements and trends that are shaping the future of the violin:

Advancements in Violin Making

Modern luthiers are using cutting-edge technology and scientific analysis to create violins that push the boundaries of sound quality.

- **3-D Printing:** This technology is being explored to create violins with unique designs and potentially even improved acoustic properties.

- **Material Science:** Luthiers are experimenting with new materials, like carbon fiber, to create lighter, stronger, and more weather-resistant instruments.

The Rise of the E-Violin

The electric violin has come a long way since its humble beginnings. Today, these instruments offer a vast array of tonal possibilities, allowing violinists to explore genres like rock, pop, and electronica.

- **Beyond Amplification:** Modern electric violins go beyond just amplifying the sound. They can be equipped with effects pedals to transform the violin's sound entirely, opening doors to creative sonic exploration.

- **Breaking Barriers:** Electric violins are making classical music more accessible to new audiences. It's not unusual to find a rock concert featuring a soaring electric violin solo alongside a traditional orchestra.

Violins Around the World

The violin isn't just for fancy concert halls anymore. It's traveled the world and become a part of countless musical styles. Here's a glimpse at some exciting examples:

- **Bluegrass:** The violin is a star player in the toe-tapping bluegrass genre. Its high-pitched melodies combine the banjo and guitar, adding a sweet and sharp sound to this fast-paced music.

- **Irish Fiddle:** This lively style features a special type of violin called a fiddle. Its bright, clear tone perfectly complements the lively jigs and reels of Irish dancing.

- **Indian Classical:** Violins, called veenas in India, play a vital role in Hindustani classical music. They sing long, soulful melodies that bend and twist in beautiful ways.

- **Rock and Pop:** Violins aren't strangers to rock and pop. From Led Zeppelin's "Stairway to Heaven" to Lindsey Stirling's electric violin performances, the violin adds a touch of elegance and power to modern music.

Genre-Bending Fusion

The future of the violin is a fusion of styles and traditions. Here are some exciting trends to keep an eye on:

- **World Music Fusion:** Violinists are increasingly incorporating elements of world music traditions into their playing, creating exciting new sounds that bridge cultures.

- **Violins and Technology:** The line between acoustic and electronic music is blurred. Violinists are using technology like looping pedals and synthesizers to create unique sonic landscapes.

- **Collaborative Spirit:** The future of music is about collaboration. Expect to see violinists working with musicians from all backgrounds, creating music that defies categorization.

The future of the violin is bright. With innovative instruments, creative musicians, and a spirit of exploration, the violin is poised to continue captivating audiences for generations.

Wow, you've traveled through time and learned all about the violin's amazing history, from its early beginnings to the modern marvels you see today. You've met some legendary violinists and discovered some of the most iconic violin pieces ever composed. The violin's journey is far from over, and who knows, maybe someday you'll be part of its future. Keep exploring, learning, and playing your violin with pride. After all, you're not just a musician; you're part of a long and exciting tradition.

Conclusion

Great job, rockstar. That's a wrap on violins. You've conquered the basics (and maybe even some not-so-basics) of the amazing violin. You've jammed through necessary skills, from learning about the violin's history to making it belt out epic tunes. Now, it's time for a quick recap before you unleash your inner violin master on the world.

Key Takeaways

- **Violins Rule:** Made from fancy wood, these beauties can express a whole range of emotions, from making you cry happy tears to headbanging like a rockstar (depending on the music, of course).

- **Getting Started:** Picking the right size violin, rocking a comfy posture, and mastering that bow hold are the secret weapons that will make you a violin pro.

- **Practice Makes Progress:** It takes time and dedication to become a violin master. Learning bowing methods, mastering tricky finger placements, and practicing regularly are your golden tickets to violin mastery. Celebrate your wins, regardless of how small, and find music that makes you want to jump for joy.

- **Music Unlocks:** Reading notes might seem like a secret code at first, but you'll crack it in no time. Mastering scales will make your fingers fly on the fingerboard, and tackling tougher pieces will build your musical arsenal and make you a confident player.

- **Violin Care 101:** Your violin is your best bud, so treat it with respect. Keep it clean, store it in a cool, dry place, and take it to the violin doctor for checkups. Doing these things will keep your violin singing proudly for years to come.

- **A Musical Time Machine:** Violins have an interesting history and are played in all music genres. From fancy classical music to rock with electric violins, exploring these different styles will make you appreciate the violin's versatility and inspire you to find your musical voice.

Did this book help you kick off your violin journey? Do you have any questions or awesome tips to share with other violin enthusiasts? Leave a review below and tell others about your violin adventures. As you close the final page of this guide, prepare to embrace the challenges, and let the music flow from your violin. Keep practicing, exploring, and creating beautiful sounds that will rock the world.

References

Anon. (2019, March 15). Learn the Violin By Yourself: The Ultimate Guide. Violinspiration. https://violinspiration.com/the-ultimate-guide-to-learn-the-violin-by-yourself/

Armin. (2023, June 29). Violin Basics: The Complete Beginner's Guide. Violinspiration. https://violinspiration.com/violin-basics/

Lora. (2023, April 11). Learn to Play Violin in 20 Steps. Meadowlark Violin Studio. https://meadowlarkviolin.com/violinblog/learn-to-play-violin-yourself-20-steps

Mastering the Violin: A Comprehensive Guide to Bowing Technique | Trala. (n.d.). Www.trala.com. https://www.trala.com/resources/violin-bowing-technique

Termeer, J. (2021, May 5). All 25 Violin Bowing Techniques with Examples & Symbols. Violinspiration. https://violinspiration.com/violin-bowing-techniques-terms-symbols-and-definitions/

traithar. (2023, May 17). 10 Best Violin Bowing Exercises for Beginners. Violinspiration. https://violinspiration.com/violin-bowing-exercises/

Violin Online - How to Hold the Violin. (n.d.). Www.violinonline.com. https://www.violinonline.com/howtoholdtheviolin.html

Printed in Dunstable, United Kingdom